THE INCAS

THE

INCAS

BY BARBARA L. BECK
Revised by
LORNA GREENBERG

A First Book/Revised Edition
FRANKLIN WATTS
New York/London/Toronto/Sydney/1983

Frontispiece:
a pottery vessel of the
pre-Inca Nazca culture.

Map courtesy of Vantage Art, Inc.

Cover illustration: A fifteenth-century
woven Inca tunic, with a design of crouching
catlike creatures, perhaps pumas.
Courtesy of the Metropolitan Museum of Art.

Interior photographs courtesy of
The Metropolitan Museum of Art: pp. frontis, 7, 8, 22;
American Geographical Society Collection of the University
of Wisconsin, Milwaukee: pp. 2, 11, 23, 39, 44;
United Nations: pp. 14, 18, 30, 31, 35, 51, 57;
American Museum of Natural History: pp. 26, 40, 46;
Peruvian Tourism Promotion Fund: p. 54.

Library of Congress Cataloging in Publication Data

Beck, Barbara L.
The Incas.

(A First book)
Previously published as:
The first book of the Incas. 1966.
Bibliography: p.
Includes index.
Summary: Discusses the Inca civilization and
its downfall at the hands of the Spaniards.
1. Incas—Juvenile literature. [1. Incas.
2. Indians of South America]
I. Greenberg, Lorna.
II. Title.
F3429.B4 1983   980'.004'98   82-17657
ISBN 0-531-04528-5

CONTENTS

THE INCAS

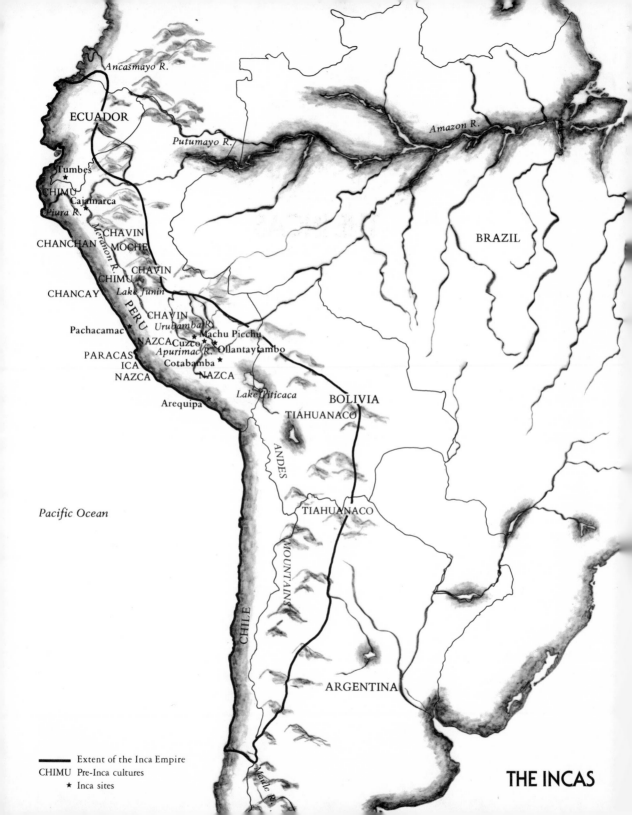

Ancasmayo R.

ECUADOR

Putumayo R.

Amazon R.

Tumbes ★

CHIMU

Cajamarca ★

Piura R.

CHANCHAN

CHAVIN

MOCHE

Marañon R.

CHIMU

CHAVIN

CHANCAY

Lake Junin

PERU

CHAVIN

Urubamba R.

Pachacamac ★

NAZCA Cuzco ★ ★ Machu Picchu

Apurimac R. ★ Ollantaytambo

PARACAS

ICA

Cotabamba ★

NAZCA

NAZCA

Lake Titicaca

Arequipa ★

BOLIVIA

TIAHUANACO

BRAZIL

Pacific Ocean

ANDES

TIAHUANACO

MOUNTAINS

CHILE

ARGENTINA

Maule R.

─── Extent of the Inca Empire

CHIMU Pre-Inca cultures

★ Inca sites

THE INCAS

1

DISCOVERING
A CIVILIZATION

The early Spanish explorers of the New World had carried back to Spain fantastic tales—of a marvelous golden land of unbelievable wealth. No one could say just where to find this unseen land, which came to be called Peru. It was always somewhere "to the south." In 1524 an illiterate but fiercely determined Spanish adventurer scraped together enough money for a ship and a crew, and set sail for South America. This was Francisco Pizarro's first attempt to find the golden cities of the explorers' tales. On a later voyage, he finally reached a small city called Tumbes, or Tumbez, on the edge of a mysterious civilization. So in 1532, the European world, in the person of a rugged, single-minded adventurer, gained its first glimpse of the wonders of the mighty Inca Empire.

The land of the Incas spread from the present-day cities of Quito in Ecuador to below Santiago in Chile. It included parts of what are now Ecuador, Peru, Bolivia, Chile, and Argentina.

Peru, the homeland of the Incas, has three kinds of country: coastal deserts pierced by river valleys, high mountains, and dense jungles. The river valleys of the coastal desert were settled in the days before the Incas by many Indian tribes. The mountains, the Andes, were the home of the Incas and other, earlier, peoples. In the jungles to the east of the Andes lived savage tribes. The coastal desert and the mountains to the edge of the jungle became the realm of the Incas.

Archaeologists and other scientists continue to study the Inca
civilization to try to understand its mysteries—
such as these amphitheaters outside the Inca city of Cuzco.

2

FINDING OUT ABOUT THE INCAS

Learning about the Incas, and about the people who lived before them—the pre-Inca civilizations—is hard, for none of these peoples developed a written language. For the earlier civilizations, most of what we know has been collected through the work of archeologists. These scientists carefully studied every trace left by early people—in their tombs, temples, and roads, in villages and in trash heaps. The information they gained has been used to create a picture of the Andean world, from the first millennium B.C. through the time of the Inca Empire. As study continues and new finds are uncovered, the archeologists, historians, and other scientists of today will add to the picture.

From the time the Spanish arrived and began their assault on the Incas, we have other sources of information. There are journals, diaries, reports, and histories describing the Inca world. These were written in Spanish, some by soldier-secretaries or officials of the conquistadores (the Spanish "conquerors"), some by Catholic priests who came to convert the Indians, and finally, some by Spanish-educated, half-Inca, half-Spanish writers. These writings are colorful, exciting sources of information. But they are personal accounts and are sometimes unfair or inaccurate, and harshly judge the Incas, seeing them only from a Spanish view.

[3]

Pedro de Cieza de León was a young boy in Spain who was fascinated by the magnificent gold objects brought back to King Philip by the first conquistadores. In 1535, when he was only about fifteen, he sailed forth to join the Spanish forces. He spent seventeen years traveling some 3,000 miles (4,800 km) through South America, and his diaries provide many details of Inca life. He described everything he saw and heard—the customs and beliefs of the Incas, their myths and history, the plant and animal life of the region, Indian cures, farming methods, military tactics, and even gossip.

Another writer, Garcilaso de la Vega, called "el Inca," was born in 1539 of a royal Inca mother and a noble Spanish father. When he was twenty he left Peru for Spain where, many years later, he wrote a history of the Inca people: *The Royal Commentaries of the Incas.* The book contains interesting, but not always accurate, information about Inca legends, customs, and conquests.

Another Spanish-Inca author, Felipe Guamán Poma de Ayala, who worked from 1560 to 1599, created illustrated accounts of Inca life. His pictures often appear in modern books about the Incas.

Following these early books, there have been a number of careful studies by more recent historians. In 1847 William H. Prescott published *History of the Conquest of Peru.* This classic, highly valued book was followed by Sir Clements Robert Markham's *A History of Peru.*

In 1911, Hiram Bingham, an explorer, discovered the famous Inca stronghold of Machu Picchu, high in the Andes Mountains. His book, *Lost City of the Incas*, tells the story of his search. Bingham's companion, Philip Ainsworth Means, wrote *Ancient Civilizations of the Andes* and *Fall of the Inca Empire and the Spanish Rule in Peru, 1530-1780.* John Hemming's *The Conquest of the Incas*, published in 1970, is a careful and interesting history that includes a great deal of new information.

3

PERU BEFORE
THE INCAS

Thousands of years before the great Inca empire, wandering hunters lived in both North and South America. They may have reached the Americas by crossing over a natural bridge of land that once connected Alaska and Asia. Perhaps they were following the herds of wild animals that provided them with meat for food, skins for clothing and bones for making simple tools.

Gradually, small groups of the hunters formed settlements. In the Andean region, from the earliest days of settlement (perhaps 5000 B.C.), the pattern has been for people to form self-sufficient independent communities—each providing its own food and building its own social organization.

At first the people relied on food from the Pacific Ocean and on wild plants and animals. Then the Indians learned that seeds would produce plants, and they began to cultivate crops. By 2500 B.C., the Indians grew gourds, to cut into bowls and other utensils, and squashes. Depending on the soil and on the climate where they lived, different groups later grew a great variety of crops: beans, peanuts, chili peppers, avocados, mangoes, bananas, and more. Indian corn (maize), potatoes, and cotton became the most important.

As early as 3000 B.C. some communities had advanced far beyond the early hunter-gatherers and the early farmers. The people lived in true towns, with large populations. They built temples and tombs. They made fabrics and some ornaments. The making of pottery was a later skill and developed after 2000 B.C.

In time, a good number of independent and varied civilizations were thriving in the Andean region, strung along the fertile river valleys of the coastal region and tucked into the rugged highlands. Some of the most important were the Chavín, the Paracas, the Nazca, the Mochica, the Tiahuanaco, and the Chimu. The names we use to identify these cultures are taken from the names of river valleys, peninsulas, or some other landmarks of their home region.

The Chavín was a strong civilization that flourished in northern Peru and on the central coast from about 1200 to 400 B.C. The ruins of the city of Chavín de Huántar, in a narrow valley of the Andes, show the people were clever architects and artists. Their fine stone carvings, pottery, textiles, and metalwork often picture a fierce, catlike god—perhaps a puma or a jaguar. Their powerful art style spread through large areas of Peru and sometimes Chavín designs and figures displaced local gods and styles.

The Paracas civilization, which was centered on the south coast from about 900 B.C. to A.D. 400, was influenced by the Chavín. The Paracas adopted Chavín mythical figures, but they also developed their own style, to be seen in their brightly painted pottery and beautiful fabrics. The fabrics were woven on looms, from cotton and from wool from the alpaca. Because they were important in the elaborate burial customs of the Paracas, the fabrics have been preserved. The Paracas Indians prepared their dead with great care. They placed them

A catlike creature appears in nearly all designs of the Chavín culture—on carved walls, in fabrics, in hammered gold ornaments, and on pottery vessels.

[6]

in sitting positions, then wrapped each one in many layers of cloth. Clothing and ritual objects were inserted between the layers. The large bundles were put in underground chambers and covered with logs and sand. Some chambers held dozens of mummy bundles buried one on top of another. Coastal Peru's hot sun raised the temperature in the underground tombs to that of an oven. The heat dried everything and so the cloth wrappings were preserved. The colored wrappings, ponchos, breechcloths, cloaks, and hats are some of the finest fabrics ever found in the Americas.

The Nazca, whose time of strength was from about 500 B.C. to A.D. 600, succeeded the Paracas and lived a little to the south of them. The Nazca, too, wove fine fabrics, but their glorious pottery, painted in many beautiful colors, was their greatest achievement. Nazca designs included birds, fish, fruit, and strange mythological creatures.

The Nazca region is also known for the mysterious lines and figures these people cut out of the earth. The patterns, which they made by scraping away the earth's stony brown crust to show the yellow sand underneath, can be seen only from a great height. Some of the lines are 5 miles (8 km) long. While we can't know what these lines and patterns may mean, some scholars think they were used for astronomical studies, perhaps as a basis for a calendar.

The Mochica flourished on the north coast, in the Moche River valley, from about A.D. 100 to 750. These people were great practical inventors and many of their ideas were later adopted by the Incas. They developed irrigation systems with canals and aqueducts. They fertilized their fields with guano, the droppings of a coastline bird, and

Mochica pottery showed realistic portraits and scenes, and also mythical creatures like this finely detailed vessel with the head of a deer and a warrior's body.

today guano is still used in Peru. They built roads through their empire, maintained armies, and developed a messenger system where runners carried messages marked on beans. Near today's city of Trujillo, there still stand ruins of their two great pyramid shrines—the Temple of the Sun and the Temple of the Moon. As perhaps their most lasting gift to us, Mochica pottery provides an encyclopedia of the Mochica world. They modeled pots in the shapes of their birds, animals, gods and houses and of people engaged in every activity of life. Other pots show painted realistic scenes of war, hunting, thieves being punished, surgeons operating on patients, chiefs receiving gifts, and much more.

Sometime around A.D. 500, a group of people from the southern highlands began to influence the civilizations along the coast. The invaders' art style, which we now call the Tiahuanaco, seems to have spread suddenly. It brought to the coast the religion of the "weeping god," who was pictured with "tear bands" around his eyes.

The center of the Tiahuanaco culture was on the bleak *altiplano*, or "high plain," of Bolivia, nearly 3 miles (5 km) high. On this cold, dreary plain the ruins of Tiahuanaco can still be seen. One ruin was a fortress built on a step-sided pyramid. It is called the Acapana. A huge rectangular structure called the Calasasaya had an inner court and a great doorway now known as the Gateway of the Sun. The Puma Puncu, or Lion's Gate, is another platform structure of huge stones, some of which weigh 100 tons. There are remains of cutout stone seats, staircases, statues, and altars.

The Tiahuanaco style was short-lived in the coastal lands. Even so, it left its mark. For many years coastal pottery and weaving showed the weeping god, pumas, condors, and snakes in the Tiahuanaco way.

When the Tiahuanaco influence began to fade, many small nations again sprang up along the coast of Peru. The Chimu, dating from about A.D. 1000 to 1466, is the best known. The Chimu kingdom was an outgrowth of the Mochica empire and included about 600 miles (960 km) of coast, roughly from present-day Lima to Ecuador. Chanchan was the capital.

Encircled by thick, 50-foot (15.1-m) high walls,
the Chimu capital of Chanchan was a magnificent
city of temples, fortresses, homes, workshops, and
palaces—like this one seen from the air.

Chanchan was a carefully planned city of 14 square miles (36 sq km). It had enormous pyramids, walls as high as 40 feet (12 m) and a maze of sheltered streets, houses, terraces, and cemeteries. Chanchan's engineers built irrigation systems and huge stone-lined reservoirs. The city was built of large adobe bricks—blocks of sun-dried mud. Adobe will last for centuries in a dry, sunny climate, but Chanchan is in ruins today because of freak rainstorms which have washed away most of the adobe.

The clay walls of Chimu cities, and of others built in the same period, are covered with designs. These small, intricate designs—some geometrical, others of birds and fishes—were arranged in patterns that were repeated over and over again.

Only people with a strong central government could have built such grand cities as Chanchan. It would take a strong government to organize the large labor forces and to direct them.

While the kingdoms of the coast were thriving, a handful of Indians in and around Cuzco were beginning to gather strength. In less than one hundred years they would build an empire and would rule over all the coastal and highland peoples.

4

THE COMING OF
THE INCAS

The early days of the Incas are clouded by myths. When we try to trace their beginnings, we can find few facts. We do know the Incas were one of the many small tribes, or family groups, who were living in the highlands of Peru before the thirteenth century. They spoke a language we call Quechua (KESH-wa). Sometimes before A.D. 1200, they moved into the Cuzco Valley.

But Inca legends tell a more colorful story of their origins. In the beginning, everything was dark. Then Viracocha, "Lord of Beginnings," came forth and created heaven and earth. He created, too, a race of people. When they began to quarrel, Viracocha was angered and turned the people to stones. These are the great stones found at Tiahuanaco, near the southern shore of Lake Titicaca.

Sometime later, Viracocha, the creator god, reappeared from the waters of Lake Titicaca and put the sun and the moon in the heavens. Then, from the living earth, he created new tribes of people and sent them out—to all corners of the world—telling them where to live.

In legend, Viracocha is described as a very tall man, with a great beard, and dressed in long white robes. Some stories tell how he traveled among all his tribes to show the people how to grow plants, organize their governments, and lead good lives. He taught them languages, customs, and even dances. When he had finished, he reached

*On Lake Titicaca, legendary birthplace of the first Incas,
today's Indians still make Inca-style boats
from the totora reeds that grow on the edges of the lake.*

the edge of the Pacific Ocean. There he held out his robes and was carried off above the surface of the water, leaving behind a promise, some legends say, to return if his people needed him. The name Viracocha, or "foam of the sea," is a reminder of how he was borne away, across the tops of the waves.

Another legend tells how Inti, the sun god, created four brothers and four sisters. They emerged from a window in the earth—a cave. Ten families of followers emerged from two caves alongside. The children of the sun god and their followers set out to find a homeland. When one brother proved troublesome, the other three walled him up in a cave. Later, two other brothers were turned to stone. Only one brother, Manco Capac, was left—to become the founder of the Inca nation.

Inti, the sun god, had given his children a staff of gold. They were to settle where the staff of gold would sink deep into the earth. Manco Capac and his sisters and their followers wandered northward until they reached a beautiful river valley circled by mountains. Here, when Manco Capac threw the golden rod, it disappeared into the ground. In this place they founded a city and named it Cuzco, the "navel of the world."

Manco Capac drove out the other Indian tribes who were living in the valley. He and his sister-wife, Mama Ocllo, built a hut with a thatched roof on the spot where the future Temple of the Sun was to rise.

So the Inca dynasty began with Manco Capac, the first Inca, about 1200. Legends say that Sinchi Roca, son of Manco Capac and Mama Ocllo, was the second Inca leader. His name, Sinchi, means "warrior chief." In all, there were thirteen Inca rulers until the time of the Spanish conquest. But for the first two hundred years of the Inca nation—through the reigns of the first eight Incas—history and legend are twisted so closely that it is hard to know what is true. During this time the Incas settled into life in the Cuzco valley. There were frequent battles against neighboring tribes, but the Inca nation remained a small, struggling state. That was to change with the coming of the ninth Inca—Pachacuti.

[15]

5

HOW THE EMPIRE GREW

According to legend, Viracocha Inca, the eighth Inca ruler, had a son he did not like. This young prince was a troublemaker, and his father exiled him to a llama ranch far from Cuzco. A few years later the fierce Chanca tribe sent a powerful army to attack the Inca capital. Frightened, Viracocha Inca and his family fled from Cuzco. However, the exiled prince returned with a small force and, helped by (legends say) an army miraculously formed from the rocks of the fields, defeated the Chancas. In 1438 the prince became the ninth Inca and took the name of Pachacuti—"he who transforms the earth."

Pachacuti was a great military leader and a skilled statesman. Under his rule the Inca Empire began a rapid expansion. Pachacuti seemed determined to unite the tribes and peoples of the Andean region into one powerful, unified state.

When Pachacuti, and the later Inca rulers, set out to conquer a tribe, they would first send ambassadors to the enemy, to explain the great advantages of joining the Inca world. The ambassadors spoke of how the Inca people enjoyed peace and plenty, with storehouses to provide food in times of famine. They described the fine cities and roads, and the proud Inca history. Sometimes a tribe agreed to accept Inca rule, thus avoiding a battle. Others were persuaded by the sight of the strong Inca army. But some tribes had to be conquered by force.

As soon as an enemy tribe surrendered, the great Inca state took over, to make it part of the empire. Inca soldiers were stationed there. Inca officials, called *curacas*, were sent in. The *curacas* had a census taken and divided the fields and herds in the Inca manner. The people were taught Quechua, the Inca language, and the Inca gods were set over the local gods. The sons of royal and noble families were sent back to Cuzco to learn Inca ways and loyalty to the Inca state. Idols of the local gods were also sent to Cuzco. Both the idols and the sons of the local leaders served as hostages; as long as they were in Cuzco, under Inca control, the people were afraid to rebel. If they angered the Incas, their gods and princes would be punished.

If tribes were stubborn about accepting Inca rule over their lives, large groups or even whole villages were moved to the Inca homeland. They were replaced in the conquered land by loyal Inca subjects called *mitimaes* (mit-i-MAH-ays). The *mitimaes* set a good example for the conquered tribe and taught them Inca ways. When the Inca needed soldiers, a call was sent out to all the far corners of the realm. Groups of young men from throughout the empire were recruited. They had all been trained to fight from childhood, and had weapons and equipment ready.

Their weapons were simple. The bola consisted of a number of stones, each tied to a thong. All the thongs were then tied together. When the bola was thrown, the thongs would wrap around the enemy's legs, stopping him in his tracks. Slings were used for hurling rocks. A sling was made of a thick woolen-braid or fiber rope, often 6 feet (1.8 m) long. A wide middle section held a rock. An Inca soldier gripped the two ends of the sling and whirled it over his head until it gained speed and force. Then he released one end, to hurl the rock at his enemy. In hand-to-hand fighting, the Incas used stone-headed clubs, battle-axes, and spears, and double-edged wooden swords.

For protection the Incas wore quilted cotton shirts and fastened shields of wooden slats over their backs. Each group of soldiers wore wooden or woven-cane helmets in their own special style. They carried shields made of brightly painted wood or toughened deer hide. When the soldiers attacked fortified places, a great sheet of heavy

*At Tambomachay—a ritual Inca bathing place near Cuzco—
water still flows into the stone-lined basins and pools.*

cloth was held in front of them. This could protect about one hundred men from slingstones.

The Incas were experienced in war, and their captains were clever leaders. Their tactics included setting ambushes, making brush fires, and pretending to retreat in defeat but returning at dawn to surprise the enemy.

The army marched over the fine Inca royal roads to the beat of hide drums and the music of clay, bone, or reed flutes, and clay or conch-shell trumpets. They were well equipped and well fed, for food storehouses were spaced a day's march apart all along the royal roads.

By the use of force, threats, or persuasion, the empire under Pachacuti's rule spread from Lake Titicaca in the southeast to Lake Junin in the northwest. In 1463, Pachacuti's son, Topa Inca, took charge of the army. Father and son worked together and the empire grew even larger.

Topa Inca and his army moved northward almost to present-day Quito, in Ecuador, and then turned down the coast, where he persuaded the powerful Chimu people to join the empire. He drove further south to Pachacamac, below present-day Lima. His father, Pachacuti, stayed in Cuzco to organize the ever-growing empire and to rebuild the capital.

In about 1471, Pachacuti retired and Topa Inca became the ruler. He continued his conquests of the southern coast of Peru and the northern parts of what are now Bolivia, Argentina, and Chile.

In 1493, Huayna Capac became the eleventh Lord Inca when his father, Topa Inca, died. He conquered the highlands of Ecuador, beyond Quito.

Under Huayna Capac, the empire reached its peak. It stretched over 2,500 miles (4,000 km), from north to south, and covered 380,000 square miles (984,000 sq km). Perhaps as many as twelve million people, who spoke about twenty different languages and belonged to a hundred independent tribes or groups, were now part of one great state — with one ruler, one religion, and one language.

6

THE INCA STATE

Looking back, it seems that the Inca state must have been an efficient machine. At the top was the Inca, the "divine" ruler, "the direct descendant of the sun." Below the Inca there were two classes of nobles. The higher, more powerful class was made up of the "Incas by blood." This group included all members of the ruling Inca's family and everyone else who could claim to be a direct descendant of the founding Incas—Manco Capac and Mama Ocllo. The Council of Nobles (a governing body something like the president's cabinet) was drawn from this class. "Incas by blood" served as advisers to the emperor, as high administrators, and as governors of the provinces of the empire.

The lower class of nobles were "Incas by privilege." They were given the honorary title of Inca by the ruling Inca, although they were not truly Incas by birth. These nobles were the *curacas*. Leaders or chiefs of conquered tribes or territories, and military heroes were often made *curacas*. They served as local officials, responsible for specific areas or groups of people in the empire. Their posts were inherited, and their sons were sent to school in Cuzco to gain their loyalty and to teach them Inca ways.

All the nobles dressed like the Inca, although their clothing was not as fine, and it was worn more than once. Their earlobes were pierced, like the Inca's, so they could wear golden earplugs. The slits were not as large as the Inca's, but they were still large enough to pass an egg through. (When the Spanish first saw the nobles they called them *orejones*, or "big ears.") Nobles were permitted to use litters and carry parasols—two signs of their high position.

Traditionally, the highland Indians lived in groups called *ayllus* (I-loos). An *ayllu* was a subtribe, or a small community of related families who lived alongside each other in an area and shared everything—lands, crops, animals, beliefs, and loyalties. When the Incas developed their tightly organized empire, where every person, house, field, and animal was kept track of, the *ayllus* were preserved and fitted into the Inca system.

The Incas generally followed *ayllu* ties, so they remained the basic social units of the Inca world. The government counted and divided the people of the empire into groups of, usually, ten families who were led by one family head. This leader, or foreman, was the lowest official in the Inca structure. Ten foremen reported to a *curaca* (official) who was in charge of one hundred families. Above this official was a *curaca* responsible for one thousand families, and above him was a higher-ranking *curaca* responsible for ten thousand families. So it went, up the ladder, multiplying by tens. At the top the nobles reported to the governors of the four quarters of the Inca empire. The governors were members of the Inca's council.

Every year the *curacas* took a census of the population under their control. The people were then classified, by age and sex, into twelve groups. The kind and amount of work each person was to do was clearly stated. For example, boys from nine to sixteen worked as shepherds for the llama herds; girls from nine to twelve collected plants and herbs to use for dyes and medicines. At sixty, a man retired from other work and was expected to do light tasks such as keeping rabbits and ducks, and weaving ropes.

Able-bodied men from twenty-five to fifty were called *purics* (POO-riks). The *purics* did the main work of the empire—farming, serving in the army, and working for the Inca in many other ways.

The Inca ruled many aspects of the people's lives. Every year,

Left: this slit-neck tunic of woven cotton fabric is covered with colorful featherwork designs of people, llamas, and a snake. Above: at Ollantaytambo, these ruined buildings clinging to the mountainside may have been houses for the "Chosen Women."

government officials toured the villages of the empire to select the most intelligent, ablest, and prettiest girls of about ten. These were sent to a conventlike school in Cuzco, to learn cooking, weaving, and religion. They were called "Chosen Women," and after a few years some became wives or concubines to nobles and high officials. Others became "Virgins of the Sun" and were sent to various temples. They wove garments for the priests, prepared ritual food and drink, and performed ritual dances.

Except for these young girls, all the common people were expected to marry. When the boys of a village reached twenty, and the girls sixteen, all those who had not chosen mates were lined up in two rows. A state official then paired them off. The marriage ceremonies were simple, but were followed by a great feast with much drinking and dancing.

Under Inca law the two greatest crimes, punishable by death, were disobedience to the ruling Inca and treason. There was also a heavy penalty for stealing. Since nearly everything, except for a few personal belongings, was owned by the state, stealing was a crime against the government. Laziness was considered a form of stealing because it robbed the Inca of the working time due him.

Inca officials served as judges. If a thief could convince the judges that he stole from need, they punished the authority who had overlooked this need. This authority had not done his job properly.

There was little need to steal during Inca times, however, for the state made sure that everyone shared equally. There was no poverty. When crops failed—as they sometimes did—the Inca's storehouses were opened, and food and clothing were given to the people. The *purics* did not grumble about working the Inca's fields because they knew that during hard times he would take care of his subjects.

7

WORKING FOR
THE STATE

In a society as highly organized as the Inca state, the government—the
Inca and his court, the nobles, the many officials and administrators—
and the priesthood must be supported by the people. In modern days,
people pay taxes to support the state. The Incas had no money system,
so they paid taxes through their work.

The Inca people paid two kinds of tax. The *mit'a* (MEE-ta) was a
tax of public service. The Inca ordered people to work a certain number of days on state projects: building roads and bridges; serving in the
army; laboring in gold and silver mines; serving as *chasquis* (CHAZ-
kees), or runners, who carried messages over the royal roads; or other
public work. Some tribes in the empire had special tasks assigned to
them as their *mit'a*. Men from the province of Rucana carried the
Inca's royal litter. The Canari tribe supplied men to be his bodyguards.
The Chumpivilca furnished court dancers or jesters.

The basic tax paid by the people was an agricultural labor tax. All
the farmland in the empire was divided into three parts: the people
worked one part for the government; one part for the support of the
priests and religion; one part for their *ayllu*, or community.

Each season all the villagers worked the fields of the gods first.
Next they worked the Inca's lands (for the government). Last, the
peasants worked their own share of the *ayllu's* fields. In the highlands,

DEPOCITODELINGA
COLLCA

topa ynga
yupanqui.

admiministrador
suyoyoc
apo poma chaua

depocitos del ynga

como

the herds of llamas and alpacas were also divided into three parts. When *purics* were called away to perform *mit'a*, their work was taken care of by the rest of the *ayllu*.

Every year a government overseer redivided the lands of the *ayllu* according to the peasants' needs. If a family had a new baby, they were assigned more land. If a son married, some land was taken away. The newly married couple were given one *topo* (TOO-POO) of land—a strip about 150 feet (45 m) by 300 feet (90 m). After that, an extra strip was given for the birth of a son, and one-half strip for a daughter.

Artists, craftspeople, and other workers with special skills were not required to work in the fields, as they were government employees and were supported by the state.

To count all his people and keep track of what they produced, the ruling Inca employed many accountants, or statisticians, called *quipu-camayocs* (KEE-POO-KAM-a-yuoks). The *quipu* (KEE-POO) was the Inca counting device. It had one thick main string with a series of other strings of various colors and thicknesses attached. By making knots on the *quipu*, a *quipucamayoc* could record how many people lived in a certain province, or how much corn was stored away, or many other things. The *quipu* was based on the decimal system, counting in units of ten, and was a kind of record, though the Incas never developed true writing.

This sixteenth-century drawing by Poma de Ayala shows the quipucamayoc, or quipu-reader, counting off the record of goods stored in the warehouses to the listening Inca.

THE INCA AND HIS COURT

The Inca was the head of the empire and of the imperial court at Cuzco. The term "the Inca" first meant the children that Inti, the sun god, created. It later came to mean the ruler, or emperor. Today we also use it to mean all the people of the Inca empire.

The Inca had many wives—often several hundred. His chief wife was the *coya*, or empress. Among the later Inca rulers it became the custom for the Inca to take his sister as *coya*. In this way, the sun's children were kept apart from other people.

The Inca or, if the Inca had died, the council of nobles chose a successor from among the Inca's sons. The boy chosen was usually the most promising son of the *coya*, but there was no law stating who was to succeed an Inca. This was a weak point in the system and sometimes led to conflict between rival heirs to the throne.

When the Inca died, his body was mummified. Often some of the dead Inca's servants and wives volunteered to die too, so that they could accompany their lord. The new Inca fasted for three days in a house built especially for the occasion. Then he was adorned, or crowned, with the *borla*, the Inca sign of royalty. The *borla* was a headband of multicolored cords with a row of small gold tubes that dangled over the forehead. From these tubes hung the imperial red woolen fringe—the *maskapaicha*.

[28]

A great feast followed the crowning of the new Inca. It lasted for days. A palace was built for the new ruler because the old palace now held his father's mummy.

The walls of the Inca's palace were plated with sheets of gold and silver. One room contained the throne, probably a low, red wooden stool covered with a beautiful cloth. Garcilaso de la Vega writes, however, that this stool was of solid gold and that it was placed on a raised platform of gold. Aside from this stool there was very little furniture in the palace.

The Inca carried a star-headed war club made of gold. His clothing was like that worn by the common people, but was woven of fine vicuña wool, and each garment was worn only once. In his earlobes the Inca wore huge golden earplugs decorated with jewels. He ate and drank from gold and silver plates and cups. Besides the llama meat, vegetables, potatoes, and bread eaten by the peasants, the Inca was also served wild duck, frogs, snails, fish, and tropical fruits. Any food or drink left over from a meal was placed with that day's clothing, to be saved and ceremonially burned once a year. The Inca slept on the floor on a quilted cotton mattress, under blankets of fine wool.

The Inca rarely walked. On his inspection tours of his empire he was carried from place to place on a gold-plated litter, shaded by a canopy of gold that was encrusted with jewels. Two or three hundred litter bearers went along to prepare the way ahead and to relieve bearers when they became tired.

The Inca ruled over his empire from Cuzco. At first, Cuzco was just a handful of stone huts. But as the empire expanded, it grew and each Inca ruler added to its beauty and riches.

At the spot where Manco Capac and Mama Ocllo built their house, there later rose the Temple of the Sun. This became the most important and most magnificent shrine in the empire. Here was built the Coricancha, the "golden enclosure." Stone walls enclosed a group of temples including the Temple of the Sun and shrines to the moon, the stars, and the god of thunder and the rainbow. Inside the temple dedicated to Inti, the sun god, there was an enormous gold disk—the sun image. The rays of the morning sun fell on this disk and reflected

The mighty stone walls of the hilltop fortress
of Sacsahuamán guarded Cuzco from attack.

On a street in modern Cuzco, Inca stone
walls still stand—as the massive base
for structures built by the Spanish.

through the whole shrine. The Temple of the Moon contained a similar disk of silver.

The *Villac Uma* (wil-lac oo-ma), or high priest, lived at Coricancha. Only members of the Inca's family and a few important priests could enter its sacred walls.

According to Cieza de León, the shrines of the Coricancha were grouped around a fountain made of gold and a garden of gold cornstalks, which held golden ears of corn with silver tassels. The walls of the enclosure were plated in gold, and the grass thatching on the roof was mixed with golden straws.

After the Spanish conquest, the church and monastery of Santo Domingo were built on top of the stripped Inca shrines. But in 1950 an earthquake destroyed the church and some of the Inca structures underneath were uncovered.

In the area of the Incas' palaces was the Inca school—the *yachahuasi*, or "teacher's house." Here Inca princes and sons of nobles from all parts of the empire were sent for four years, to be educated in Inca ways and prepared to take their place in the Inca state. The *amautas*, "wise men," taught them history, religion, science, military tactics, the Quechua language, and use of the *quipu*.

Ancient Cuzco, capital of the Incas, was divided into two parts: lower Cuzco, or Hurin, and upper Cuzco, or Hanan. Besides Coricancha, lower Cuzco included the palaces of the rulers and the homes of the nobles. On the narrow streets there were many houses of finely cut, polished, and fitted stone. Upper Cuzco contained the peasants' houses, which were more crudely built than those in lower Cuzco.

Four main roads led from the capital. At first they merely went short distances, to the small villages of hostile tribes. In the early years of the Incas, until 1438, the ambitious "Children of the Sun" were often at war with their neighbors. But by the time of the ninth ruler, Pachacuti, the roads led long distances to the four quarters of the Inca realm. These quarters were called the Collasuyu, or southeastern quarter; the Antisuyu, or northeastern quarter; the Chinchasuyu, or northwestern quarter; and the Cuntisuyu, or southwestern quarter. These four quarters account for the Incas' name for their empire: Tahuantinsuyu, or "Land of the Four Quarters."

9

THE INCA
PEOPLE

The Inca people were highlanders who lived in the Andes Mountains. Today the Indians in this area still live and look much as their ancestors did five hundred years ago.

Highland Indians are short in stature and stockily built. The men average 5 feet, 3 inches (160 cm), in height. The women average 4 feet, 10 inches (147.3 cm). The Indians' skin is usually coppery in color and their eyes are dark. They have high cheekbones and straight black hair. Like many Indian peoples, Inca men had little hair on their faces. They did not shave but pulled out the hair with tweezers made of shells and later of metal. In the highlands the Indians developed barrel-shaped chests and large lungs, which enabled them to take in more air than usual with every breath. This helps make up for the lack of oxygen in the atmosphere at such high altitudes. Cuzco is almost 12,000 feet (3,600 m) above sea level, and the Inca empire spread over areas that were above 16,000 feet (4,800 m) high.

Highland Indians have great strength and stamina. Without stopping for breath, they can walk miles with a hundred-pound (45-kg) load strapped to their backs.

The clothes of the common people were simple, usually woven of llama or alpaca wool or cotton from the coast. Each person had two sets—a plain one for every day and a more colorful, decorated outfit for festivals. The amount of decoration depended on a person's importance in the community. Men wore loincloths held around the waist by a woolen belt. They also wore sleeveless tunics—straight, shirtlike garments that reached their knees. A cloak of alpaca wool was added on cold days and was also used as a blanket. No Inca man set off for the day without strapping a small pouch over his shoulder. In this bag he carried some personal possessions, including magical charms and sometimes coca leaves for chewing.

Women wore ankle-length tunics with woven belts. Metal pins held them at each shoulder. They also wore woolen cloaks for warmth. Men and women wore sandals or walked barefoot, just as Peruvian highlanders do today.

Tribe members could recognize each other by their hairstyles. The Inca ruled that each tribe or province must wear its own style, with whatever combs, ribbons, or other ornaments were customary. Men usually cut their hair in bangs, while women parted their hair in the center and let it hang down, sometimes in two braids.

Day-to-day life was simple and hard. The members of a household rose early and ate a meal that was frequently made up of leftovers from the day before. Then the men and women began their day's work, most often in the fields.

After the workday, the farming families returned for a meal, usually a soup or stew. At times it was made of boiled corn and chili peppers, cooked with herbs. Sometimes strips of sun-dried llama meat, called *charqui* (CHAR-kee), were boiled with *chuñu* (CHOO-nyoo), or dried potatoes and other vegetables to make a thick soup. Guinea pigs and ducks were occasionally eaten. Corn was ground and made into dough. This was cooked as dumplings in the stew, or dropped into hot ashes and baked. Corn was also eaten on the cob.

In the last hours of daylight, the men repaired their tools, and the

An Indian woman of today uses a traditional spindle to spin fibers into thread.

women made *chicha* beer, often from corn. First they chewed the corn, then they spat it into a jar of warm water. The mixture was left to stand until it fermented. At high altitudes, where corn could not grow, the beer was made with quinoa or oca.

Besides working in the fields and taking a turn at guarding them at night, the women had many other tasks. They cooked, kept house, ground corn, raised their children, and spun thread and wove clothing for their families.

The people's homes were small and simple, usually a rectangle of stone held together with mud, or else of blocks of adobe. The roofs were thatched with grass. There were seldom any windows and only one low doorway. The "door" was often just a stick or woolen curtain. Usually the people cooked outdoors, over a wood fire ringed by low stones. When they did cook inside, they used a stone or clay fireplace, and the smoke escaped through the thatched roof. The floor was pounded-down earth, upon which they put their blankets when it was time to sleep. Animals, including guinea pigs and dogs, scurried in and out of the huts. On the walls there were pegs to hold clothing and slots or niches for idols.

Inca children learned by imitating their fathers and mothers. Boys learned farming and llama herding. Girls learned weaving, cooking, and other household duties. When young boys came of age, in their early teens, a festival was held in the *ayllu*. Girls were given a family celebration. At their celebrations both boys and girls were given new names and new clothes. Each person had several names during a lifetime. They were given names at birth, received nicknames, and new names at their coming-of-age ceremony.

The hardworking Inca people probably had very little time for fun and games, though archeologists have found objects like dice, balls, tops, and dolls.

FARMERS AND HERDERS

The Incas were marvelous farmers. They used and improved on farming skills developed by earlier peoples of the Andes. They were able to produce more food than they needed, and harvested the largest variety of crops in ancient America.

The Inca farmers built steplike terraces up the sides of mountains to increase their farmland. They created impressive irrigation systems, with canals, tunnels, and aqueducts, to provide water for their crops. They made their land more fertile by the use of fertilizer, especially guano—the droppings of an offshore bird that were collected and distributed throughout the empire.

Highland crops included corn, beans, potatoes, squashes, peppers, tobacco, quinoa and oca. Quinoa is a plant with many tiny seeds that the Incas boiled, or ground into a meal. The underground tubers of the oca were cooked until they made a thick porridge. The Incas grew dozens of varieties of potatoes—a plant they developed from bitter, nut-sized tubers.

At very high regions, over 12,000 feet (3,600 m), the Incas could do little farming. Potatoes were the main food here. They were preserved by being allowed to freeze and then thaw. Next, the Incas would trample them to force out the water. After drying in the sun, this food was called *chuño* (CHOO-nyoo).

Along the coast of Peru, and in the valleys, many more crops were grown, including tomatoes, cotton, tropical fruits, cacao (chocolate), and peanuts.

At the start of the planting season there was a festival and then everyone came out to work the soil. Even the Inca ruler arrived with a golden spade and began the ceremony by turning over the first piece of earth. Nobles and other officials also worked for a short while, but they soon stopped, leaving the peasants to carry on.

The ground was broken with a long-handled wooden spade, called a *taclla*. The men formed lines and dug, working backward. The women followed, on their knees, breaking each clod of earth into loose soil. Next the men made holes in the ground with a planting stick. Again the women followed, dropping grains of corn into the holes. According to custom, the women did the sowing because it was believed that seeds would not come up otherwise.

After the planting, the rainy season was anxiously awaited. If there was no rain, the people dressed in mourning and walked, weeping, through the villages. Sometimes they tied up a black llama or a dog until it died from hunger and thirst. The people hoped the animal's cries would soften the hearts of the gods so they would send rain for the crops.

On the barren and windy high plateaus, where few crops could be grown, the Incas raised herds of llamas and alpacas. The Indians had bred these animals from the wild guanaco (hwan-A-co). The llama and the small alpaca both supplied wool for clothing, and the llama also provided meat and hides. Llamas are stubborn and bad-tempered, like their relative, the camel. No one rides them for they balk at carrying a person's weight, but they can transport loads of under a hundred pounds (45 kg), and can travel for miles without water. They were the only pack animals in Peru until the Spanish brought their horses.

The wild guanaco and the vicuña (vi-KYU-nya) are also related to the camel. Every year the Inca ordered a roundup of the animals. Thousands of Indians gathered in the area chosen for that year's hunt. The *purics* formed a great circle and then gradually closed in, until they could hold hands. Cieza de León says that as many as forty thou-

Throughout the lands of the Inca empire, agricultural
terraces mark ridges on the mountain slopes.

sand guanacos and vicuñas were trapped within a circle. The guanacos were killed for meat, but the vicuñas were freed after being sheared of their fine wool. Vicuña wool was reserved for the use of the Inca and his court.

This alpaca was fashioned
from plates of silver
by an Inca artist.

11

THE INCA BUILDERS

The Incas' efficient system of government was probably their greatest achievement. Next were the famous Inca roads and buildings. Their amazing roads covered nearly 10,000 miles (16,000 km) to unite the empire. The Royal Road, carved out of the mountain walls, ran for 3,250 miles (5,200 km) through the high Andes. In places the road had to zigzag up mountains or tunnel behind stone cliffs, and was only 3 feet (.9 m) wide; but it formed an unbroken highway down the length of the empire.

The second major road, the coastal highway, was wide and straight—running for 2,520 miles (4,032 km) from Tumbes in the north to Arequipa in the south, and perhaps even further for hundreds of miles into Chile. Other roads crossed back and forth between these two great highways.

Since the Incas did not use the wheel, the roads were used only by pack-carrying llamas, by messengers and foot travelers who had been given permission by the government to use the highways, and by the Inca's armies.

All along the highways, spaced a day's journey apart, there were inns, or rest houses, called *tampus* (TAM-poos). Government storehouses—holding supplies for an army of about twenty-five thousand—were often built near the *tampus*. Cities along the roads also had royal *tampus*, for the Inca's use when he traveled.

[42]

Purics were called up from local *ayllus* to build the roads and to keep them in good condition, as their *mit'a*. Government engineers were sent from Cuzco to plan the roads and oversee the workers.

In many places the engineers had difficult problems to solve. They built causeways over marshes and designed different kinds of bridges to cross the mountain rivers and ravines. Suspension bridges spanned some of the widest valleys. Many of these amazing hanging bridges were still used in Spanish colonial times. One bridge, 250 feet (75 m) long, spanning the Apurimac River, lasted from 1350 to 1890.

The suspension bridges were made of five thick cables of braided fibers from the maguey (ma-GAY) plant. The cables, often as thick as a person's body, were stretched across the ravine. The ends were attached to beams that were sunk into great piles of stones and earth. Three cables held the floor of the bridge. Smaller ropes or vines laced these three cables to the other two, which served as side rails. Mud and matting were placed over the floor cables. Nearby *ayllus* were responsible for replacing the cables every year or two, as their labor tax, or *mit'a*. The bridges swayed frighteningly in the wind, but people and llamas—and later the horses of the Spanish—crossed over them safely.

The Incas also built pontoon bridges of reed boats strapped together and covered with mud and grasses. In another type of bridge the traveler would sit in a basket that hung from a cable. A bridge attendant would draw the basket across the ravine.

The runners called *chasquis* raced over the roads and bridges, taking messages and small packages from town to town, province to province, and to the Inca in Cuzco. They often carried *quipus*, the counting device of dangling strings, with information knotted into them.

Every 1 or 2 miles (1.6 or 3.2 km) along the road there were two small huts, one on either side of the track. Inside each sat two runners who waited for the arrival of a messenger. When a runner appeared, one of the waiting *chasquis* sprang up and ran alongside to receive the message, *quipu*, or package, and carry it on to the next relay station. The *chasquis* could run from Lima to Cuzco, 420 miles (672 km), in

The sure-footed flock of llamas uses an Inca-style suspension bridge to cross above a mountain river.

three days. The Inca could have fresh fish from the coast in two days, a distance of 130 miles (208 km). It seems as if the *chasquis* could run a mile (1.6 km) in six and a half minutes.

Getting from place to place easily and receiving information quickly were important to the government. If a rebellion began, the Inca could quickly send troops to stop the trouble before it spread. By the same means, enemy tribes were often surprised before they were ready to meet an Inca army.

The Incas' vast road network joined hundreds of villages and cities. The cities had nearby *pucaras* (poo-KA-ras), or hilltop fortresses. The *pucaras* were small cities themselves, with a sun temple, houses, reservoirs, and barracks for troops. If an enemy threatened, the city people fled to the protection of their *pucara*.

Perhaps the most amazing piece of architecture in the Americas is a *pucara* called Sacsahuamán. This great fortress crowns a high hill above Cuzco. It was begun by Pachacuti, but Cieza de León wrote that twenty thousand Indians labored seventy years to build it.

Sacsahuamán has three terraced walls, one above another, facing a flat plaza. The walls are over 20 feet (6 m) high, a mile (1.6 km) long, and are set in a pattern that zigzags over the ground like the teeth of a saw. The first wall has some stone blocks that are 20 feet (6 m) high, 14 feet (4.2 m) long, 12 feet (3.6 m) wide, and weigh 200 tons.

Ollantaytambo was another *pucara*, northwest of Cuzco, near the Urubamba River. This fort protected the Incas from raids by fierce northern tribes.

Farther north the Urubamba River races into a gorge. High above the river, clinging to the steep mountains lining the gorge, are a series of five fortresses, about 10 miles (16 km) apart. These forts guard the narrow mountain road to Machu Picchu, the famous stone fortress that the Spaniards never found.

Machu Picchu stands hidden some 2,000 feet (600 m) above the river, between two mountain peaks. It was discovered by Hiram Bingham, the explorer, in 1911. Machu Picchu had terraces for farming, thatched-roof houses, barracks for soldiers, and temples and palaces. Water was brought in by a stone aqueduct from springs a mile (1.6 km) away.

[45]

*The fine, polished stonework, the trapezoidal windows,
steps cut out of stone, and a simple, strong design
were all characteristics of the Inca building style,
as seen here in the round temple at Machu Picchu.*

Inside the city wall, the water was channeled to fall over steps into a series of sixteen stone basins, one lower than the other. This unique water system is called the Stairway of the Fountains. Women filled their water jars at these stone basins. This city of stone buildings has been restored. The roofs of some buildings have even been rethatched, so that today Machu Picchu looks very much as it did over four hundred years ago.

The finest Inca buildings were built of carefully cut and polished stone. No cement was used to hold the stones together. It is amazing that the Incas could build as they did, using only stone tools.

Building stones were quarried and then pulled, on rollers, to the building site. Here the stones were shaped and polished by skilled stonecutters. Each stone was then pulled up an earth ramp, by ropes, and fitted exactly to the next stone, probably by rubbing the two stones together. The fitting was so close that even today a knife cannot be slid between them.

Inca cities were planned by government architects, who first worked with small clay models. Once a plan was finished, it was used over and over again, for different cities in the empire. Each city was built by local people, as part of their *mit'a*, under government architects and overseers. Archeologists and explorers have found and studied many Inca cities. Their buildings have almost disappeared because the stones were removed by later peoples for new structures, or because trees and vines have grown up through them and toppled them.

Inca architecture had a special mark: openings in the buildings were shaped as trapezoids — they were four-sided figures that were narrower at their tops. Sometimes the windows were blind, they had no openings but were only niches. Nearly all Inca buildings have windows, niches, or doorways that are trapezoidal.

12

RELIGION, SCIENCE, AND THE ARTS

Religion, superstitions, and legends were woven deep into the people's lives. The highest Inca god was Viracocha, the creator, "Lord of Beginnings." Next came Inti, the sun god, father of the Inca rulers. Then came gods and goddesses of thunder, the earth, the moon, the stars, the sea, the rainbow, and others. The thunder god was really a weather, or rain, god. In Inca designs his sister is often shown holding a jar of water. When the thunder god wished rain to fall, he broke the jar with his slingshot. The thunderclap was the crack of the slingshot. The rainwater came from the Milky Way, a river in the skies.

The Inca ruler was believed to be the "son of the sun," and was therefore a living god. After an Inca ruler died, his body was preserved as a mummy and worshiped. At important ceremonies in Cuzco, mummies of all the dead Incas were brought out from their palaces to witness the rituals.

The Inca's favorite brother, or another close relative, was usually named high priest, *Villac Uma*, and led all great festivals. While there were temples to the sun in nearly every city, religious ceremonies were usually held outdoors.

In Cuzco and throughout the empire, there were many lesser priests who had various duties. They sacrificed llamas and sometimes guinea pigs to the gods. In a time of great trouble, a child or young person was sacrificed. The priests also heard confessions, interpreted oracles, and cured sick people.

Religious festivals marked every month of the twelve-month Inca year. In December the people celebrated *Capac Raimi*—"magnificent festival"; *Pauca Huaray*, in March, honored "earth ripening"; *Inti Raimi*, in June, was the "festival of the sun."

At these festivals the people danced, drank chicha beer, joined in footraces, sang, and played musical instruments. The instruments included tambourines, bells, drums made from hollow logs with tight deerskin covers, trumpets made from seashells or baked clay, flutes made from the bones of animals, and panpipes made of reeds or clay. In their dances, farmers acted out their daily chores, or soldiers went through the motions of a battle to the rhythm of the music.

Besides the official gods, the people worshiped *huacas* (WAK-as), or "sacred shrines." Cuzco, where the Inca state was founded, was a *huaca*; Pachacamac, on the coast of Peru, with a famous oracle, was also a *huaca*. People made pilgrimages to these two sacred places. Some stones, springs, mountains, caves, tombs, temples, palaces, and other objects were also *huacas*. Each was believed to be the home of a spirit who must be kept in good humor. A special type of *huaca* was an *apachita* (a-pach-EE-ta), a pile of rocks at a dangerous turn in the road. Here travelers prayed for safety on their journey and then cast a stone, a piece of old cloth, or something else onto the *apachita*.

Soothsayers or fortunetellers were members of the priest class and interpreted signs and omens. Soothsaying was often done by casting pebbles or corn kernels on the ground, or by watching what turn a snake took or how llama fat burned in a fire. Twitching eyelids, the howl of a dog, or a fire that suddenly flared up—all had special meaning to diviners and to the common people.

The Incas believed that sickness was usually caused by sorcery or the ill will of other people, or by gods who had been angered. So illness was treated by magic and by religion. Sometimes a medicine man, or sorcerer, was supposed to "remove" a troublesome object from the patient's body, as a cure. To do this, the medicine man waved his hand over the patient. Soon the object, a pin or stone, appeared in his hand.

The patient was thus made well. Curing was accompanied by prayers, offerings to the gods, and sometimes by a ceremonial bathing in a nearby stream.

In addition to this belief in sorcery and magic, the Incas understood a good deal about medicine and surgery. Various plants were used in treatment: cocaine, from the coca plant, was used to relieve pain; belladonna was used for eye ailments; resin from a certain tree healed wounds.

Incas performed an operation on the skull called trepanning. When a warrior received a severe blow on the head he was probably given coca (cocaine) or some other drug to deaden the pain. The surgeon then operated to remove any broken pieces of bone that pressed on the brain. Trepanning may also have been performed as a ritual. Many surgical instruments have been found in Peruvian graves: scalpels, knives, needles for stitching up wounds, and pincers. Tourniquets, used to stop the flow of blood, and bandages have also been found.

In addition to medicine, the Incas had some knowledge of astronomy. They had a twelve-month calendar. Each month lasted thirty days, divided into three ten-day weeks. Then there were five days in the year left for festivals. The Incas based their calendar on observations of the sun from four stone towers built by Pachacuti, to the east and west of Cuzco.

The artists of the Incas produced fine weaving, metalworking, and pottery. Women did nearly all the spinning, and they wove cloth on looms, using wool from the alpaca, llama, and vicuña, and cotton from the coast. They used a backstrap loom. One end of the loom was tied to a tree or post, while the other end was tied to a band around the weaver's back. By moving back from the tree, the weaver could tighten the threads on the loom. This kind of loom could not produce cloth more than 30 inches (26 cm) wide — about the span of the weaver's arms.

Dyes were made mostly from plants: indigo for blue, achiote for red. Along the coast, shellfish were used for dying fabrics. The Incas grew cotton in a variety of natural shades, ranging from white to rusty-brown to gray.

*In Indian villages women continue to weave richly patterned
fabrics on looms similar to those used by the Incas.*

Inca potters made pitchers and jars with pointed bases, called *aryballuses* (ar-y-BAL-lus-es). Each jar had a knob around which a rope could be wound for carrying purposes. The pottery was painted with red, white, and black, and sometimes yellow and orange, in small geometric patterns. Besides pottery, the Incas used flat-bottomed stone dishes and wooden drinking cups called *keros.*

Gold was used only by the Inca ruler and the nobles. It was often pounded into thin sheets and used for plating the walls of palaces or temples. Masks, earplugs, goblets, plates, statues, and ceremonial knives were also made from both gold and silver. Some tools and weapons were made from copper and bronze.

According to Garcilaso de la Vega, Huayna Capac, the eleventh emperor, had a chain of gold 700 feet (210 m) long. It was used in a ceremonial dance in the great square at Cuzco. Each link was as big as a man's wrist, and the chain was so heavy that two hundred Indians had difficulty in carrying it. This chain, if it ever existed, was never found by the gold-loving Spaniards.

13

THE SPANISH CONQUEST

Toward the end of Huayna Capac's reign a strange rumor came to the royal court in Cuzco. The Inca's armies had marched south to put down an uprising. They discovered that the rebellious Indians were accompanied by a strange-looking man who was white and wore a beard. This Spanish adventurer had been shipwrecked on the coast of Brazil and later had been captured by the Indians. He was the first European to be seen by the Incas.

Other reports came to Huayna Capac about pale men in "sea houses," or ships. Finally thirteen white men landed at Tumbes. This was the first Spanish expedition to the land of the Incas. Huayna Capac did nothing, and the Spanish soon left.

In 1525, Huayna Capac died during an epidemic which may have been smallpox or measles. (Both of these diseases had been brought to South America by the Spanish.) He died before he could choose which son was to follow him as Inca. One son, Atahualpa, ruled the north and lived in Quito. Another, Huascar, ruled the south from Cuzco. The two brothers reigned for some time, but suspicion, treachery, and ambition filled their hearts. Atahualpa had his father's great army, which was still at Quito, following an earlier campaign. War broke out, and Atahualpa sent his father's army against Huascar. This civil war was to last for several years and tear the empire apart.

Huascar's army marched north to meet that of Atahualpa at Riobamba. The fierce battle was won by Atahualpa's forces, as were several others. Triumphant, Atahualpa moved his troops south to make his headquarters at Cajamarca. Huascar again set out to meet his brother's troops. Finally at Cotabamba, a town not far from Cuzco, Huascar's soldiers were ambushed in a ravine and slaughtered. Huascar himself was captured, and his men fled. The victorious army camped on the outskirts of Cuzco. Atahualpa, the new Inca ruler, ordered that all members of Huascar's family be executed and that Huascar be imprisoned. He was later killed by order of Atahualpa.

At the time of Atahualpa's victory, there were rumors of a second appearance of white men on the coast. He decided to stay away from Cuzco until these strange people left, as they had five years before.

In May, 1532, one hundred and eighty Spanish foot soldiers and cavalrymen had landed above the coastal city of Tumbes. Their leader was the ambitious, fearless Francisco Pizarro, who sought gold and power. Pizarro knew of the war between the two brothers. With sixty-two horsemen, one hundred and six infantry soldiers, and a few small cannon which shot stone balls, he marched toward Cajamarca. On November 15, 1532, this tiny army entered the deserted city. The Inca and a force of thirty thousand men were camped on the plains outside Cajamarca. It is believed that Atahualpa expected the Spaniards to surrender.

Pizarro sent two captains, Hernando de Soto and Hernando Pizarro, his brother, with thirty-five horsemen to Atahualpa's camp to arrange a meeting. The Incas had never before seen horses, and when de Soto galloped his horse toward Atahualpa some of the Inca's men

*Machu Picchu—called the
"Lost City" of the Incas—
is carved into a mountain
ridge 2,000 feet (606 m)
above the Urubamba River.*

shrank back in fear. The horse was pulled up just inches from the Inca, who never flinched. It is said that afterward Atahualpa beheaded those who had shown fear. The emperor agreed to meet the Spanish commander the following day.

The following afternoon the Inca, seated on a throne of gold borne by nobles, approached the city with five thousand men. Pizarro's men were hidden around the great square. When Atahualpa entered, this square was empty. He asked, "Where are the strangers?" and his attendants answered that the Spaniards were afraid.

The Spanish priest, Valverde, approached the Inca party. With him was an Indian boy who spoke Spanish and Quechua. Valverde explained that Spain and its king were now rulers of the land. He held out a prayer book to Atahualpa, but according to some historians the Inca threw it to the ground.

A shot was fired and the Spanish battle cry, "*Santiago*" filled the square. Spanish crossbows, cannons, and muskets rained death on the bewildered Indians. Atahualpa was dragged from his golden litter and made a prisoner, while his army fled in terror. Over two thousand Indians were killed.

After his capture, Atahualpa realized that, most of all, the Spanish wanted gold. He tried to ransom himself by promising Pizarro enough gold and silver to fill his cell as high as his hand could reach — over 7 feet (2.1 m). Pizarro agreed, and word went out to every corner of the empire. For two months, gold and silver poured into Cajamarca on the backs of llamas and people, until the line drawn high on the wall was reached.

Inca goldsmiths were kept busy for over a month melting down beautiful gold and silver works of art. The metal was then cast into bars. One-fifth of the ransom was set aside for Charles V, king of Spain. The rest was divided among Pizarro's men. It has been estimated that the value of Atahualpa's ransom today would be about sixty-five million dollars.

Although the Inca was declared free, he remained a prisoner. The Spanish were afraid of an uprising and soon decided that it would be safer if he were killed. Atahualpa was given a choice: if he accepted

Here at the giant hill fortress of Ollantaytambo, Manco Inca and thousands of Inca warriors lined the stone terraces to fight off a Spanish attack in the last days of the Inca empire.

Christianity, the Spaniards would strangle him rather than burn him at the stake. If he were burned, his body would be destroyed, and could not be mummified and returned to Cuzco. So he accepted Christianity. The last Inca ruler was strangled and died in the summer of 1533.

For years after Atahualpa's death the Inca people, led by Manco Inca, a half brother of Huascar, and by his sons, tried to restore the empire. But the Spanish forces grew stronger and the Inca people gradually lost their will to fight. Finally Topa Amaru, leader of a band who still resisted the Spanish, was executed in Cuzco in 1572.

Within a span of less than one hundred years, from the time of Pachacuti to Atahualpa, the Incas forged a great empire of perhaps as many as twelve million people. But the efficient, successful state toppled almost overnight. Without the Inca at the top to rule, the whole structure of the state collapsed. The loss of authority, the civil war that bled the country and loosened the ties of empire, and the plagues of measles, influenza, and smallpox all weakened the empire. And so, a small band of Spanish adventurers was able to achieve the ruin of a mighty empire—the golden land of ancient America.

THE INCA RULERS

Manco Capac (A.D. 1250*)
Sinchi Roca
Lloque Yupanqui
Mayta Capac
Capac Yupanqui
Inca Roca
Yahuar Huacac
Viracocha Inca
Pachacuti (1438*–1471*)
Topa Inca (1471*–1493*)
Huayna Capac (1493*–1527)
Huascar (1527–1532)
Atahualpa (1527–1532)

*Approximate dates

CHRONOLOGY

1200*	The Incas enter Cuzco.
1400*	Viracocha Inca becomes the ruler.
1438*	Pachacuti becomes emperor.
1463*	Topa Inca commands the army.
1471*	Topa Inca succeeds his father to the throne.
1492	Columbus discovers America.
1493*	Topa Inca dies and is succeeded by Huayna Capac.
1511*	Huayna Capac goes north to battle the Indians of Ecuador.
1513	Balboa discovers the Pacific Ocean.
1524–25	Francisco Pizarro's first voyage.
1527*	Huayna Capac dies.
1527	Pizarro reaches the coast of Peru.
1530	War of the two brothers, Atahualpa and Huascar.
1532	Pizarro returns to conquer and loot coastal region of Peru.
1532	Atahualpa is captured.
1533	Atahualpa is killed.

*Approximate dates.

FOR FURTHER
READING

Bierhorst, John. *Black Rainbow: Legends of the Incas and Myths of Ancient Peru*. New York: Farrar, Straus and Giroux, 1976.

Blassingame, Wyatt. *The Incas and the Spanish Conquistadores*. New York: Julian Messner, 1980.

Karen, Ruth. *Kingdom of the Sun*. New York: Four Winds Press, 1975.

Leonard, Johathan Norton. *Ancient America* (Great Ages of Man). New York: Time-Life Books, 1967.

McIntyre, Loren. *The Incredible Incas; and Their Timeless Land*. Washington: National Geographic Society, 1975.

INDEX